By and By

By and By

CHARLES ALBERT TINDLEY
the Father of Gospel Music

Carole Boston Weatherford

ILLUSTRATED BY Bryan Collier

atheneum

ATHENEUM BOOKS FOR YOUNG READERS

NEW YORK LONDON TORONTO SYDNEY NEW DELHI

$\mathcal{A}$
atheneum

ATHENEUM BOOKS FOR YOUNG READERS

An imprint of Simon & Schuster Children's Publishing Division

1230 Avenue of the Americas, New York, New York 10020

ATHENEUM BOOKS FOR YOUNG READERS is a registered trademark of Simon & Schuster, Inc.

Atheneum logo is a trademark of Simon & Schuster, Inc.

For information about special discounts for bulk purchases, please contact Simon & Schuster Special Sales

at 1-866-506-1949 or business@simonandschuster.com.

The Simon & Schuster Speakers Bureau can bring authors to your live event.

For more information or to book an event, contact the Simon & Schuster Speakers Bureau

at 1-866-248-3049 or visit our website at www.simonspeakers.com.

Book design by Laurent Linn

The text for this book was set in Cantoria MT Std.

The illustrations for this book were rendered in watercolor and collage.

Manufactured in China

1019 SCP

First Edition

2 4 6 8 10 9 7 5 3 1

Library of Congress Cataloging-in-Publication Data

Names: Weatherford, Carole Boston, 1956- author. | Collier, Bryan, illustrator.

Title: By and by : Charles Tindley, the father of gospel music / Carole Boston Weatherford ; illustrated by Bryan Collier.

Description: First Edition. | New York City : Atheneum Books for Young Readers, 2020.

Identifiers: LCCN 2018055626 (print) | LCCN 2019018902 (eBook) |

ISBN 9781534426375 (eBook) | ISBN 9781534426368 (hardcover)

Subjects: LCSH: Tindley, Charles Albert—Juvenile literature. | Methodist Church—Clergy—Biography—Juvenile

literature. | Hymn writers—United States—Biography—Juvenile literature. | Gospel music—History and criticism—

Juvenile literature.

Classification: LCC BX8473.T54 (eBook) | LCC BX8473.T54 W43 2020 (print) | DDC 287/.6092 [B] —dc23

LC record available at https://lccn.loc.gov/2018055626

In memory of my grandfather, the Reverend Lun P. Whitten
—C. B. W.

I dedicate this book to Reverend Frank Tyson, Joan Merritte, Stiles and Brenda Paterson,
and all the members of the Tindley Temple family. I'd like to thank you for sharing your
time and oral history about this great man of faith and music, Reverend Charles Tindley.
—B. C.

My life is a sermon inside a song.
I'll sing it for you. Won't take long.

Berlin, Maryland, 1851,
Charles and Hester had a son.
Father, enslaved, but Mother, free;
The law spared me from slavery.

A little tyke when Mama died;
Can't remember if I cried.
Raised by an aunt, no Mama's arms;
Minding masters, hired out to farms.

I think of children with parents at home . . .
While mine are gone and I am alone.

Chants in the field at break of dawn.
Keep yo' han' on-a dat plow. Hold on!
Hold on!

Spirituals, first Bible that I heard.
I yearned for more—to read the Word.

Newspaper scraps lit by glowing pine knots.
Lines of type absorbed my thoughts.

Keep your lamps bright and burning
And your vessels filled with oil.

Letters and words like tiny seeds
Bloomed to life as I learned to read.

Patched work pants and wrinkled shirt,
Barefoot, trekked five miles to church.

Beams of heaven, as I go
Through this wilderness below,
Guide my feet in peaceful ways,
Turn my midnights into days.

The church folk were all wearing shoes.
My soiled feet hid beneath the pews.

The preacher nearly called my name.
He asked, "Who reads? Be not ashamed."

He beckoned children down the aisle.
My journey seemed one hundred miles.

I've been 'buked an' I've been scorned.
I've been talked about, sho's you're born.

My heart raced as I held the book.
My palms were wet and my voice shook.

But as I read the Bible aloud
I had never felt so proud.

And when my verse came to an end,
The church folk nodded, said, "Amen!"

I've slippers in the Kingdom.
Ain't that good news!

I vowed to learn one thing each day,
Trusting God to lead my way.

Farmhand by day, student by night,
Miles to trek to read and write.

As years went on the more I yearned
For time to quench my thirst to learn.

I married Daisy after the war.
We moved to Philly, wanting more.

Two jobs, long hours, to keep us fed.
At night I dreamed of books I'd read.

Night school; then God's call to preach.
Was the cloth within my reach?

Private tutors, courses by mail,
Tests that others swore I'd fail.

Granted knowledge that God bestowed,
I passed the test and donned the robe.

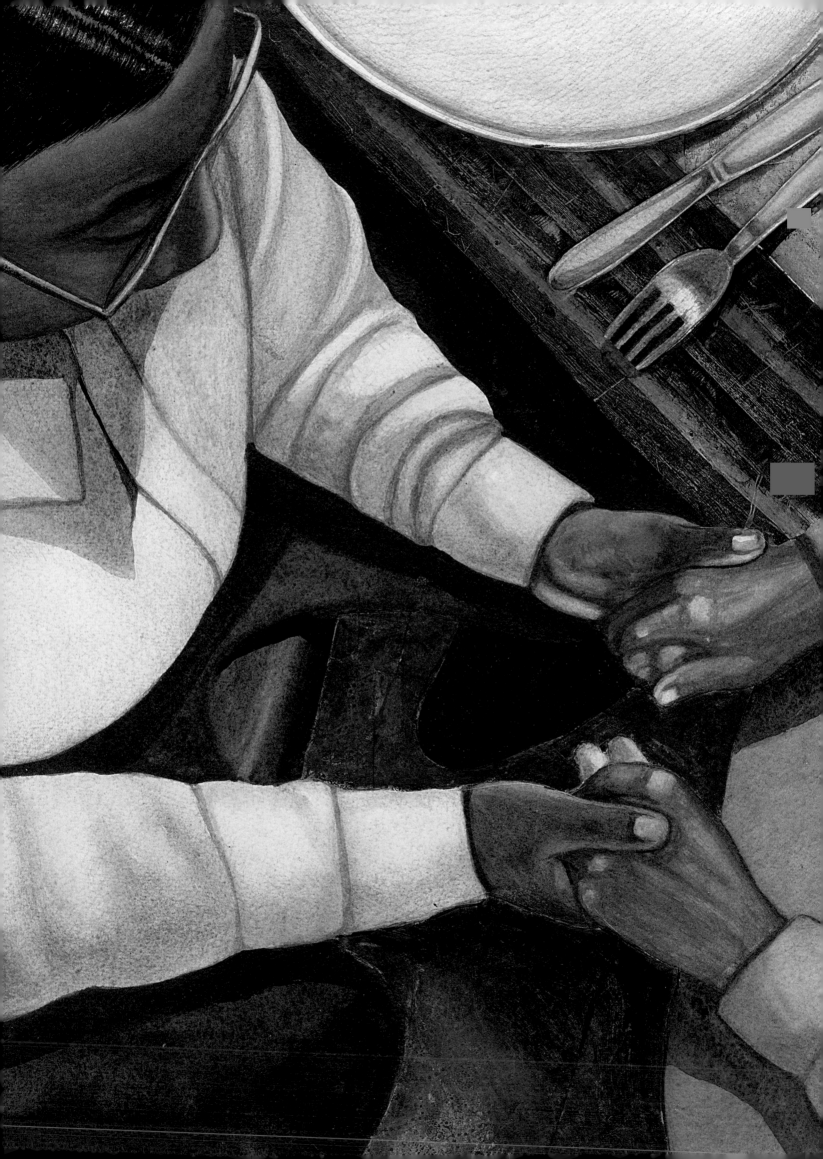

Rich in spirit but not in pay,
Our table bare, we paused to pray.

Just remember, in His Word,
How He feeds the little bird—

Knock, knock: neighbor brought a meal,
Proving miracles are real.

Every Sunday, eleven o' clock,
I fed a growing, hungry flock.

I still heard spirituals of long ago,
Remembered how they moved me so.

Hardships woven into hymns I wrote—
Every lyric, every note.

When I do the best I can,
And my friends misunderstand,
Thou who knowest all about me,
Stand by me.

Uphill road, then an open door
To pastor where I'd scrubbed the floor.

Fleeing harsh discrimination,
Thousands northbound—Great Migration.

Factory jobs, a shot that's fair.
A better home . . . I'm going there.

Instead of pay they'd hoped to earn,
Big-city blues at every turn.

Nation gripped by the Great Depression.
Hungry masses starved for blessings.

With open hearts and open doors,
My church fed and clothed the poor.

We even offered families loans,
Helped them purchase their first homes.

We are taught to love each other,
And as one should treat a brother,
We must do by one another.

Over time, my small flock grew:
Fifteen thousand in the pews.

Children filled the balcony.
Their beaming faces lifted me.

Mid-sermon I'd burst into song,
My voice encircling the throng.

Weeknights I led praying bands.
Believers singing, clapping hands.
The storm is passing over, Hallelujah!

We formed a book club to uplift,
An orchestra to nurture gifts.

I wrote a hymnal—*Soul Echoes*—
Mostly songs that I composed.

As if penned by God's own hand,
My hymns rang out across the land.

Though I began as my own teacher,
I was crowned the "prince of preachers."

The church I led now bears my name;
My songs, an everlasting flame.

"I know the Lord will make a way."
And I'll overcome someday.
Amen!

AUTHOR'S NOTE

Charles Albert Tindley was born in 1851 to an enslaved father and a free mother who died when he was very young. Tindley was just seven when his father hired him out to live and work alongside farmhands and enslaved people. The African American spirituals that Tindley heard in the fields introduced him to Bible stories.

Forbidden by his employers to have books, Tindley used newspaper scraps to learn the alphabet and spelling. Later, after working all day, he'd walk seven miles for lessons from a schoolteacher. By age seventeen, Charles could read and write.

As a young man in Philadelphia, Pennsylvania, Tindley worked as a brick-layers' helper, went to school at night, and bought every book he could. He took courses by mail, at a Hebrew synagogue, and with private tutors.

In 1901, Tindley began composing hymns that drew on his faith and everyday experiences. The composer of dozens of hymns, he was truly the father of gospel music.

In 1902, Tindley became pastor of East Calvary Methodist Episcopal Church, where he had once been janitor. Sunday mornings, worshipers packed the 3,200-seat sanctuary to hear him preach. Known as the "people's pastor" and the "prince of preachers," he started a soup kitchen and clothing ministry that continue today. In 1927, his church was renamed Tindley Temple. Tindley died in 1933.

When Tindley died, he left a rich musical legacy. His best-known songs include "We'll Understand It Better By and By," "Leave It There," "The Storm Is Passing Over," and "I'll Overcome Some Day," which inspired the civil rights anthem, "We Shall Overcome."

ILLUSTRATOR'S NOTE

I grew up on the eastern shore of Maryland in the rural town of Pocomoke City, which is about thirty miles south of the birth place of Charles Albert Tindley in Berlin, Maryland.

Doing this book was a mind-blowing experience, mainly because there was an abandoned church called Tindley's Chapel situated next to my childhood home.

Every year, Tindley Day is celebrated in our town, reminding us of the good news and the gospel and the music of Charles Tindley.

The watercolor and collage images depict the journey of young Tindley from field worker to custodial work to night school to becoming the pastor of his own church, which was later named Tindley Temple, in Philadelphia, Pennsylvania.

The art also reflects a lyrical quality, as you will see sheet music dancing throughout the book. The musical aspect expresses the emotional journey Tindley was experiencing as he struggled to grow, lead his African American flock, and provide a worshipping sanctuary.

POPULAR HYMNS BY CHARLES TINDLEY

"A Better Home"
"I'll Overcome Some Day"
"I'm Going There"
"Leave It There"
"Nothing Between"
"Beams of Heaven as I Go" (original title: "Some Day")
"Stand by Me"
"The Storm Is Passing Over"
"We'll Understand It Better By and By"
"What Are They Doing in Heaven?"

BIBLIOGRAPHY

Jones, Ralph H. *Charles Albert Tindley: Prince of Preachers.* Nashville: Abingdon Press, 1982.

Thomas, Velma Maia. *Freedom's Children: The Passage from Emancipation to the Great Migration.* New York: Crown, 2000.

Tindley, E. T. *The Prince of Colored Preachers: The Remarkable Story of Charles Albert Tindley*. Wilmore, Kentucky: First Fruits Press, 2016.

RESOURCES

Igus, Toyomi. Illustrated by Michelle Wood. *I See the Rhythm of Gospel*.
 Grand Rapids, MI: Zonderkidz: 2010.

Taylor House Museum, Berlin, Maryland.
https://taylorhousemuseum.org/history/charles-albert-tindley/.

Tindley, Charles Albert. *Beams of Heaven: Hymns of Charles Tindley*.
 Board of Global Ministries - Global Praise, 2006. (Audio CD)

Tindley Temple: A Highlight of Methodist History.
http://www.umc.org/who-we-are/tindley-temple-a-highlight-of-
 methodist-history.

Tindley Temple Historical Marker.
http://explorepahistory.com/hmarker.php?markerId=1-A-59.

Charles Albert Tindley

SONGS QUOTED IN THE BOOK

IN ORDER OF APPEARANCE

"It May Be the Best for Me" (by Charles Tindley)

"Hold On" (an African American spiritual)

"Travelers to the Heavenly World" (by Charles Tindley)

"Beams of Heaven As I Go" (original title: "Some Day") (by Charles Tindley)

"I've Been 'Buked an' I've Been Scorned" (an African American spiritual)

"Ain't That Good News" (an African American spiritual)

"I Know the Lord Will Make a Way" (by Charles Tindley)

"Leave It There" (by Charles Tindley)

"Stand by Me" (by Charles Tindley)

"I'm Going There" and "A Better Home" (by Charles Tindley)

"The Storm Is Passing Over" (by Charles Tindley)

"I Know the Lord Will Make a Way" (by Charles Tindley)

"I'll Overcome Some Day" (by Charles Tindley)